"Sister Marie's prayer-poems are real SPIRIT-FILLED gifts for prayer and reflection, bringing alive faith, hope, and love."
Rev. John E. Cockayne
Spiritual Director of Persons with Disabilities
Archdiocese of Hartford, Connecticut

"Sister Marie's prayer reflections always give me comfort and a sense of being surrounded by God's love. They have inspired me during my cancer journey especially as I cope with the effects of chemotherapy."
Janet Cekovsky, cancer patient

"The prayers, poetry, and writings shared by Sister Marie are certainly guided by the Holy Spirit. I feel God's peace as I leaf through the pages of her book while pausing to pray."
Susan Feliciano, wife of José Feliciano

"In her writing, Sister Marie repackages its healing spirit simply, in bits and pieces. May this collection of her prayers and spiritual verses be a blessing to many!"
Miriam Therese Winter, Ph.D
Professor of Hartford Seminary

MOMENTS...in the Spirit

to Pause, Ponder, and Pray

Sr. Marie Rose Roccapriore, M.P.F.

To Shiloh and Patty
With prayer and Blessings
that God's Love and
Peace surround you always,
Sister Marie

LEONINE PUBLISHERS
PHOENIX, ARIZONA

The Scripture citations used in this work are taken from the *New American Bible*, St. Joseph Edition, copyright © 1970 by the Confraternity of Christian Doctrine, published by Catholic Book Publishing Company, New York.

Published by Leonine Publishers LLC
Phoenix, Arizona
USA

ISBN-13: 978-1-942190-09-7

Library of Congress Control Number: 2014959286

Printed in the United States of America
10 9 8 7 6 5 4 3 2 1

Visit us online at www.leoninepublishers.com
For more information: info@leoninepublishers.com

DEDICATION

I dedicate this book in praise and thanksgiving to God for gifting me with so many blessings throughout my life;

to my loving parents and my brothers, who guided me on our journey of faith during my childhood years;

and to the Sisters of the Religious Teachers Filippini Community, who continue to encourage and inspire me in my ministry.

ACKNOWLEDGEMENTS

I am most grateful…

To God for providing me with various opportunities to express my prayerful sentiments through these simple poems.

To Sisters Gina Piazza and Mary Macri, and to Fathers John Cockayne, Ronald May, and Robert Rousseau, for their helpful suggestions and encouragement to pursue this project.

To Father Nicholas Melo, Pastor of St. Thomas Parish, for his prayerful support and affirmation of my ministerial endeavors.

To Susan Feliciano, Kathy Hjerpe, Janice Lautier, Tanya Malse, and Dr. Miriam Therese Winter, for their proofreading and assistance in preparing the final manuscript.

To Sonja Jelks for sharing her professional computer skills.

To Claire DeFrancesco for the illustrations on the chapter pages.

To my niece and nephew, Susan and James Smola, for their assistance with the cover design.

To everyone who shared their inspirational moments when pausing to ponder and pray with my prayer-poems on printed cards.

May God bless you in abundance!

OTHER WORKS
BY SISTER MARIE ROCCAPRIORE, M.P.F.

BOOKS

Anointing of the Sick and the Elderly: A Pastoral Guide for Home and Church, Alba House, 2187 Victory Blvd., Staten Island, NY, 10314

Caring for the Sick and Elderly: A Parish Guide, Twenty-Third Publications, P.O. Box 6015, New London, CT, 05320

Contributor to the *Catechist Magazine,* P.O. Box 49726, Dayton, OH, 45449

MUSIC

Spirit Joy, Vol. I CD (18 Songs) recorded with José Feliciano

Spirit Joy, Vol. II CD (19 Songs) recorded with José Feliciano

Spirit Joy, Vol. III CD (15 Songs) recorded with José Feliciano

Sing Blessings on America – (A Single Recording) by Spirit Joy with accompaniment by José Feliciano

DVD: *Called to Celebrate* – A live concert featuring Spirit Joy Children's Music Group with José Feliciano

Spirit Joy Songbook: A Melody and Lyric Book
Speed Print Productions, 1232 East Main Street, Meriden, CT, 06450

ONLINE

www.SpiritJoy.org

mpfmr@att.net

www.JoseFeliciano.com

www.catechist.com

CONTENTS

Healing 27

Seasonal 41

Beatitudes 51

Trust 61

Family 71

Celebrations 77

Surrender 85

Symbols 97

INTRODUCTION

The reflections in this text were written over a period of several years, and include the religious and Spirit-filled encounters experienced during various situations in my life.

Although written in diverse settings, each one manifests a yearning to unite one's spiritual and physical state with God in this busy world. The need to *pause* every now and then during a busy schedule, to *ponder* on a relationship with God in each circumstance of daily life, and to be grateful for all His blessings and special graces, prompted me to seize opportunities that would lead to a focus on the spiritual dimensions of experiences. As I attempted to connect each of the day's events with the Lord, I began to express this mindfulness in the form of little prayers. My natural enjoyment of poetry led me to express these prayers in simple poems.

The positive comments received, when sharing these prayerful reflections with family and friends, prompted me to print them on little cards for distribution to others on various occasions. They were especially welcomed by residents in nursing homes and patients in hospitals, and were used in various prayer groups and parish gatherings. I was then encouraged to extend the circulation of these reflections to a wider group of people by compiling them in book form. They are arranged according to themes and classified under ten categories: *Stillness, Gratitude, Healing, Seasonal, Beatitudes, Trust, Family, Celebrations, Surrender,* and *Symbols.*

It is my ardent hope that these simple prayers and reflections will bring inspiration to more people, and likewise prompt them to take some time to pause, ponder, and prayerfully connect with God in their diverse situations and experiences.

"Be still and know that I am God..."
Psalm 46:11

Stillness

A TRANQUIL PAUSE

Lord, amidst loud clamoring today,
I pause to catch Your sound;
Though foreign noises strain my ears,
Your Words of Love abound.

This tranquil time affords a chance
To stop and upward gaze;
Withdrawn from hurried, routine pace,
I pray in thankful praise.

Give blessing to this moment, Lord,
Renew me with Your strength;
Anoint my efforts with a joy
To praise at greater length.

Let all I think and say and do
Be tidings that ring true;
And help me share, more, what I hear
Each time I pause with You.

GOD'S FACE IN OUR CHAPEL

Oh, how blessed and graced I am, to pause in convent's place!
'Midst these wooden chairs and kneelers, I sit in sacred space.

In prayerful, peaceful stillness, through quiet time, I hear
Nature's sounds, which, often, were not heard or very clear.

God's voice, in gentle whispers, bids me to come and rest,
So energy can fill me to serve with greater zest.

Praise God for allowing me the vision of this scene,
Love's portrait, the Eucharist, framed with background of
    green.

During these reflective moments, I see God's Caring Face
And feel a holy presence of peace and healing grace.

Empowered by the Spirit, with strength to do God's Will,
Renewed, I'll journey onward, despite what binds me still.

God's blessings in abundance surround me as I pray;
God's Face of Love Eternal smiles joy along my way!

I thank the Lord for this time of special, love-filled power
And sing my heartfelt praises for gifts God sends this hour.

COLORS ARE GIFTS

So many colors beneath the sky
Remain unnoticed, and I know why.

With hurry, scurry and rush to "do"
What time is left to fathom a hue?

Yet colors teach lessons, great and small,
They tell how different one is from all.

Each carries a special tone and shade
Some lose their luster; some never fade.

God's color-gifts could be dark or light
Bearing much contrast, like black and white.

They bring significant signs of Him:
Red for God's Love and white for no sin.

Green signals hope and immortal life,
Blue: peace and calm, though there be strife.

In yellow, orange, and golden rod,
A joyous praise to the Sun of God!

Whether pastels or chromatic kind,
Colors dress moods or relax one's mind.

They beautify each day on this earth,
But haste makes easy to waste their worth.

How boring life's scenes would surely be
If just one color we'd always see!

Thank You, Lord, for slowing this minute;
To notice Your signs of love in it!

I praise You for these beautiful gifts,
Your colors, our sacramental lifts!

GOD'S LOVE

If I climbed the highest mountain,
    Or plunged into the deepest sea,
I could never really fathom
    The love God has for me.

If I walked in flower gardens,
    Or drove on city streets,
I would pass all kinds of love-signs
    That focus on God's treats.

If I were all alone in space,
    Or 'midst a noisy crowd,
God's love would be no different,
    But echo clear and loud.

If I would fail and fall quite low,
    Away from grace through sin,
God would keep on loving, waiting
    For me to love Him in.

It heals me just to think about
    God's great unchanging love,
And for this gift, forever new,
    All praise and thanks above!

I SEE HIM

I saw God's Face and see Him still
    So many times each day;
It seems when I am most busy
    A new cause prompts me: *pray.*

While in the midst of much to-do,
    My heart speaks: "Halt this pace.
Now lift your voice in prayerful praise
    And recognize His Face."

I thank You, Father, for Your LOVE
    To see You in this hour;
Such choicest gifts You share with me
    Reveal Your Presence-Power.

I thank You, Jesus, for Your LIGHT
    To guide me in the night;
If I should lose direction points,
    You lead the way that's right.

I thank You, Spirit, for Your TRUTH
    That truly sets me free;
Take now my life and seal me with
    Your own identity.

I thank You, Holy Triune God,
    For blessing me with grace,
To see with eyes of healing hope
    New life in someone's face.

JOURNEY QUESTIONING

What do You ask of me, Lord? What do You want me to do?
I yearn for more peace and joy, and ask for advice from You.

Where, on this personal journey, should my steps take me these
  days?
I'm confused with directions; some point to self-centered ways.

I seek to gain more joy, Lord; I'm unsure just how or where.
Speak to me now—I'll listen; this is my earnest prayer.

I'm tempted to avoid paths where the sun is out of sight;
Please take my hand and lead me to places You make bright.

I prefer to walk on pathways where life's bumps are rare or few;
Please help me to be willing to take risks for You anew.

In my travels of past years, I've walked, stumbled, and run.
Now at this venture in life, new quests for You have begun.

Please steady my limbs and gait, and add new strength to my pace
To go where others need me, to share the love of Your Face.

Forgive me for doubtful times, when my trust gave way to fear;
I'm sorry for refusing to admit Your Presence near.

Accept this prayerful searching to know and follow Your Will;
I promise to move onward with greater faithfulness still.

Anoint me, Your pilgrim, Lord; let my walk be one long praise
'Til You lead me safely home, to the realm of Your Love's Gaze.
Amen.

WHAT IS A GIFT?

A Gift is the receiving of something for free,
    And a sharing of new hope with me.

A Gift is accepting the truth from a friend
    And believing that deep cuts will mend.

A Gift is a phone call from someone who cares
    And a special remembrance in prayers.

A Gift is a letter when sick or shut in
    And being absolved of every sin.

A Gift is the time someone took to reach out,
    And encouragement when facing doubt.

A Gift is the soft touch of a sturdy hand
    And knowing someone does understand.

A Gift is a visit with no feast in mind
    And a glance that is gentle and kind.

A Gift is when hurt has been lifted above
    And forgiveness brings new depths of love.

A Gift is bread, blessed and then broken to eat
    And the taste of God's grace ever-sweet.

The Gift is God's Son, Who has come to end strife
    And His Holy Breath in my own life.

A Gift is you in whose mirror I see
    The love and joy of the Trinity.

I Gift you with His Love in me
    And pray God's choicest gifts will be
    Wrapped for you for eternity.

WHAT IS LOVE?

Love is *kindness* when it's hard to understand;
Love is *sharing* though you've a quasi-empty hand.

Love is *looking up* when trials drag you low;
Love is *pausing* though others urge you: *go.*

Love is *reflecting* when it's hurry-up-and-do;
Love is *caring* though the need is more in you.

Love is *listening* when your ears are blocked a bit;
Love is *building* though past failures bid you quit.

Love is *growing* when life-signs seem to cease;
Love is *dying* to all that destroys peace.

Love is *constant*, it's in every single minute;
Love is *God* and His blessed fullness in it.

Love is *all of us* who live our own lives true;
Love is people of *faith*, who share God's love anew.

May each of us reflect *Love's joy* and daily renew
Our prayers to be *faithful,* to keep on loving, too.

"O Lord, my God, forever will I give you thanks."
Psalm 30:13

Gratitude

A PRAYER OF THANKS

Thank You for this Call, dear God,
        To serve You all these years,
And for the grace to persevere
        'Midst laughter, pain, and tears.

Thank You for the chance to share
        Your love with young and old,
And all those opportunities
        For blessings manifold.

Thank You for Your Faithful Love
        And for community,
For family, friends, and others
        Who reached out lovingly.

Thank You for the challenges,
        The big ones and the small,
And for Your help to view them
        As part of this "love-call."

O gracious God, I thank You
        For this Anniversary Day.
May Your gift of Spirit Joy
        Forever bless my way!

A THANK YOU MESSAGE

For many acts of kindness
And gentleness each day,
And all the joy you brought me
In your own loving way,

I offer my sincere thanks
And heartfelt wishes, too.
God give a special blessing
On you and all you do!

Accept my praise-filled prayer
And let it prove to be
My way of saying "thank you,"
For being a gift to me.

A THANKSGIVING PRAYER

Lord, it's easy to give thanks to You for gifts that bring us pleasure,
For beauty that surrounds us now in ways we cannot measure;

For comforts of a cozy home, nice food and physical health,
Possession of material as well as spiritual wealth;

For love of family, relatives, and the joy that friendships bring,
For true words of affirmation, that encourage us to sing;

For many gifts and privileges in this great land of the free,
For all in life You bless us with and all that is yet to be.

But thank You for the crosses, too, which You ask us to embrace;
For lovingly supporting us with Your sacramental grace.

Though "thank you" words grow faint at times, deep down within
    our being,
We remain so very grateful for life's wonders we are seeing.

For every gift of bounteous love, our hearts and minds now raise
O Father, Son, and Spirit blest, this prayer of *Thanks and Praise*.
Amen.

A THANKSGIVING REFLECTION

Thank You for this Eucharist, Lord,
Communion gift from You,
And for Your special power
To recreate us new.

Thank You for Your special treats
That nourish all our days,
And for Your touch of love
In countless little ways.

Thank You for the chance to walk
With balance towards our goal
And for the grace-filled moments
Which strengthen heart and soul.

Thank You for our family
And friends who truly care,
And for their inspiration
Through gentleness and prayer.

Thank You for these years to live
In service, wholly Thine,
And for all Your gifts
Of blessings most sublime.

Thank You, Lord, and praise to You
Now and everyday.
Keep us always in Your hands
With child-like trust, we pray.
Amen.

IN GRATITUDE FOR WINDOWS

Praise and thanks for windows, Lord,
        And for my gift of eyes
To see Your love through them each time
        I gaze up at the skies.

Windows send Your rays of light
        To beam across my bed
So Your own touch of gentle warmth
        Can rest upon my head.

Windows show when clouds roll by
        Against their background blue,
Reminding me that trials do pass
        In time ordained by You.

Windows sometimes echo noise
        From splashing drops of rain.
Could it mean heaven's telling me
        You'll wash away my pain?

Windows invite birds to pause
        With wings from flight to nest;
I see in them Your Spirit, Lord,
        Who bids me praise through rest.

Windows tell who's fast asleep
        When day moves into night;
I see in prayerful quietude
        Your stars shine out so bright.

Without windows, I can't bring
     Your outdoor beauty near;
Let me not take for granted now
     These I've been blessed with here.

Thank You, Lord, for window gifts
     Each day bestowed on me;
They frame Your wondrous majesty
     So clear for me to see.

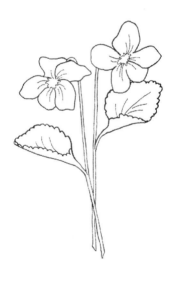

IN PRAISE OF BREAD

Today, a hurried car slowed down
    So I could take a turn in town,
And I received bread. Thank You, Lord.

My phone had rung and rung until
    The caller reached me. Was I ill?
And I received bread. Thank You, Lord.

Mom promised me a special prayer
    That God would grant me healing care,
And I received bread. Thank You, Lord.

I stood beneath a huge oak tree
    And caught a smile and wave to me,
And I received bread. Thank You, Lord.

The mailman knocked upon my door
    With things I'd long been waiting for,
And I received bread. Thank You, Lord.

I drove into a crowded place
    And someone moved to give me space,
And I received bread. Thank You, Lord.

I dropped a package in a store
    And someone brought it to my door,
And I received bread. Thank You, Lord.

A little hand reached out to mine
    To share her home-made valentine,
And I received bread. Thank You, Lord.

I saw repentance in a heart
  Where God had hardly been a part,
And I received bread. Thank you, Lord.

I needed help with a small task—
  A willing hand appeared unasked,
And I received bread. Thank You, Lord.

Mass had begun, God's Word was read.
I heard quite loud: "Take, Eat My Bread;
  In Eucharist, My Body feeds
  To satisfy all hunger needs."
And I received Bread anew. Thank you, Lord,
  for Bread is YOU!

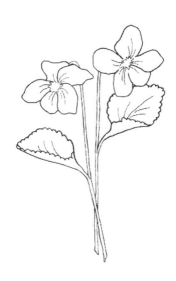

PRAISE GOD

Praise God!
> For life: to be each moment in His ever-present
> grace. For eyes: to see His image clear in every
> person's face.

Praise God!
> For strength: to keep on trusting Him when day
> seems dark as night; For giving me the faith to
> know He is my Lord and Light.

Praise God!
> For sunshine, with its soothing warmth, and for
> the drops of rain; For health that's strong, and
> ill-health, too, with grace to bear the pain.

Praise God!
> For truth—and tranquil freedom—bringing
> gladness day by day; For calling me to serve and
> render grateful praise this way.

Praise God!
> For challenging encounters, at the center of
> my life; For those of peace-filled beauty and for
> those including strife.

Praise God!
> For family, friends, and relatives, who offer
> time to share; For kindnesses expressed to me,
> especially through prayer.

Praise God!
> For Eucharistic-sharing, with His Word and Bread each day; For quietude to hear His Voice, in chapel, where I pray.

Praise God!
> For my birth and re-creation which all these years have wrought; For wonders of His goodness and for joys my *yes* has brought.

Praise God!
> For all the countless reasons, now, to utter thanks above; For saving power which comes to me through His Redeeming Love.

Praise God!

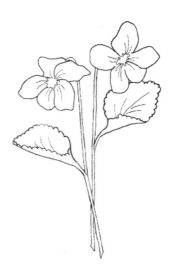

A TRIBUTE OF GRATITUDE

Thank you for those times you reached out your hand
And gently showed me you did understand.

Thank you for those times you offered your ear
And led me to trust that God's help was near.

Thank you for those times that you challenged me
Urging me to move on in Christ's Ministry.

Thank you for those times you'd quickly forgive
And bring me new hope for strong faith to live.

Thank you for those times you'd eagerly share;
That goodness in you revealed God's Own Care.

Thank you for those times a prayer came from you
And your gift brought me God's Presence anew.

God bless and keep you and fill all your days!
I pray this, my "thank you," today and always.

REFLECTION ON MARY'S IMAGE

I look at your image, Mary, and see
Love's enduring strength—womb of God;
Walk with me daily wherever I trod.

I look at your image, Mary, and see
Love's compassionate care;
Soothe all oppressed as I bathe them in prayer.

I look at your image, Mary, and see
Love's everlasting peace;
Throughout the entire world, let discord cease.

I look at your image, Mary, and see
Love's eagerness to forgive;
Bring healing hope to those striving to re-live.

I look at your image, Mary, and see
Love's faithfulness true;
May more lives mirror the image of you.

I look at your image, Mary, and see
Love's gentle, sturdy touch;
Accept my heartfelt praise, Mary:
Thank you so much!

THANK YOU, VOLUNTEERS!

Thank you for your COURAGE!
Through a YES response by you,
Christ's Word was heard anew.

Thank you for your COMMITMENT!
Through your sharing, day and night,
Christ's Love was seen so bright.

Thank you for your DEDICATION!
Through your willing hands and time,
Christ's Light was made to shine.

Thank you for your INSPIRATION!
Through your silent deeds well done,
Christ's Life touched everyone.

Know that with these THANKS today,
Come praise-filled prayers to stay.
Christ's Joy-gifts forever bless your way!

"O Lord, my God, I cried out to you and you healed me."

Psalm 30:3

Healing

ANOTHER CHANCE

Another day You give me, Lord,
Another chance to see
Your grace and love poured out anew
In measures just for me.

Another day You give me, Lord,
Another chance to mend
Those splits I have from sin and doubt,
Through pardon that You send.

Another day You give me, Lord,
Another chance to feel
Your gentle, healing power,
As it makes me more real.

Another day You give me, Lord,
Another chance to share
Your taste of Blessed Bread and Wine
In sweet Communion Prayer.

Another day You give me, Lord,
Another chance to know
Your gifts of peace and joy are mine
Wherever I may go.

Another day You give me, Lord,
Another chance to raise
My mind and heart to incense You
With prayerful thanks and praise.

Another day You give me, Lord,
Another chance to live;
Claim every moment that I breathe:
My ALL to You I give.

FORGIVE ME, LORD

Forgive me, Lord,
For all the times I failed to see
Your loving arms outstretched to me.

Forgive me, Lord,
For all the times I failed to hear
Your soothing voice dispelling fear.

Forgive me, Lord,
For all the times I failed to speak
Your words of hope to comfort the weak.

Forgive me, Lord,
For all the times I failed to bear
The treasures of Your grace in prayer.

Forgive me, Lord,
For all the times I failed to raise
My thoughts of You in thankful praise.

Forgive me, Lord,
For all the times I failed, when ill,
To recognize Your Holy Will.

Forgive me, Lord,
For all the times I failed to be
Your grateful child—Your love for me
   Is Awesome!
Forgive me, Lord!

BE FREE

Be Free...God bids me
Come and pray—let this day
Speak life *through Me.*

Be Free...
Take each loss—swiftly toss
Each one *to Me.*

Be Free...
Use your tears—to cleanse fears.
Feel safe *by Me.*

Be Free...
Feel life's pain—washed in rain
Sent now *from Me.*

Be Free...
Take My Hand—arise and stand
Secure *with Me.*

Be Free...
Hope anew—joy in you
Is trusting *in Me.*

Be Free...
Heaven's lights—break all nights
Look up and *see Me.*

Be Free...
Become whole—lose control,
Humbly *find Me.*

Be Free…
For I heal—make Faith real.
Rely *on Me*.

Be Free…Be at peace—Love won't cease;
It's stronger now
With you *and Me*. Stay Free!

CALLED TO LOVE

Every person is called by God to share gifts of love and healing. Each of us is called to be a *heart* through which love pours out, *hands* through which love heals, a *mind* through which love thinks, a *voice* through which love speaks, and a *face* through which love is visibly radiant.

While pondering the following reflection, you are invited to touch each part of the face as it is mentioned.

God calls me to be love's EYES:
>   to see new life...to see growth...to see brokenness...to
>   see tears...to see smiles...to see pain...to see recovery...
>   to see grieving...to see joys...to see love's image at
>   work.
Praise God for the gift of my eyes!

God calls me to be love's EARS:
>   To hear myself...to hear others...to hear beyond
>   words...to hear noises...to hear silence...to hear the
>   cooing of babies...to hear the sighs of the elderly...
>   to hear and to listen to the cries of the oppressed...
>   to hear with compassion and understanding...to hear
>   with patience.
Praise God for the gift of my ears!

God calls me to be love's NOSE:
>   To smell the sweet scent of blossoms...to smell the
>   stench of sickness and life turned sour...to smell
>   the fragrance of purity and godliness...to smell the
>   perfumed wax of candles dispelling darkness...to smell
>   the incense of prayer rising up to glorify God.
Praise God for the gift of my nose!

God calls me to be love's MOUTH:

> To taste the peace of forgiveness...to taste the joys of healing hope...to taste the spices of friendship...to taste the effects of honesty and integrity...to taste the special communion of caring sisters and brothers...to taste the Bread and Wine—nourishment for body and soul.

Praise God for the gift of my mouth!

Dear God, help me to be faithful in living out this call
to be love's face,
in every place,
today, tomorrow, and always.

FOR HEALTH

Heal me, Lord, with new life;

Empty me of daily strife.

Anoint me, Lord, with saving power;

Lead me to a painless hour.

Touch me, Lord, so I can live...that

Head and hands may stronger give
      service full, and cheerful, too,
      because of **HEALTH,** because of YOU.

GOD'S HEALING TOUCH

Lord, it's very dark, but I feel Your strong hand;
There's no sight ahead now, yet by me You stand.

Let the day come soon; bring me Your healing light;
Break down the thick fog of this long, dreary night.

Grant me deep courage, to brave pain without fear;
Help me to trust in Your Loving Presence here.

Touch me with peaceful surrender this hour;
Lead me to take hold of Your comforting power.

Your Love without limit brings healing to me.
I praise and thank You for listening to my plea.

I CAN

When I'm sick in bed, feeling lonely and blue,
It's easy to think of the things I can't do.

Should moments of cheer not surround me for long,
Self-pity joins weakness and sadness comes strong.

And so I make efforts to raise prayerful thoughts
By counting my blessings for all God has wrought.

In God's Loving Goodness and Almighty Plan,
When I think "I cannot," God shows me "I can."

> I cannot lift but I can hold;
> I cannot type but I can fold.
> I cannot taste but I can eat;
> I cannot cook but I can treat.
> I cannot throw but I can catch;
> I cannot drive but I can latch.
> I cannot trod but I can doze;
> I cannot stand but I can pose.
> I cannot teach but I can care;
> I cannot buy but I can share.
> I cannot sit but I can see;
> I cannot do, but I can BE.

So, when lying in bed makes me feel quite weak,
And everything 'round me seems empty and bleak,
I'll praise and thank God for strength ever-new
And try to recall all the things I CAN DO.

I FEEL GOD'S POWER

I feel God's Power in this hour, uprooting anxious fear;
The grace God sends for bodily mends assures His Presence here.

I feel God's Power in this hour, soothing life's awful stings;
God gently heeds my smallest needs, removing what hurt brings.

I feel God's Power in this hour inviting me to rest;
My silence finds a purpose—time to glorify Him best.

I feel God's Power in this hour, nourishing me anew;
In the Eucharist I'm fed with Heavenly Bread; Healing love-sign,
too.

I feel God's Power in this hour, releasing all my weight;
The cross I bear uplifts in prayer, where strength flows, ever great.

I feel God's Power in this hour, transcending time and place;
Faith's hope is gained, new joy sustained, God's Spirit fills my
space.

MY KENOSIS PRAYER

Dear God,

Empty my life of any stuff
    That brings clutter to my day;
Fill me with Your powerful grace
    To make light my pilgrim way.

Empty me of useless worry
    Which absorbs much of my time;
Fill me with a prayerful heart
    To focus on thoughts sublime.

Empty me of self-pity, Lord,
    When I moan about new pain;
Fill me with renewed energy
    To walk, unafraid of rain.

Empty me of all selfishness
    That appeals to false delight;
Fill me with a more grateful heart,
    Which praises You day and night.

Empty me of those memories
    That deprive me of true peace;
Fill me with forgiveness and love,
    So healing will never cease.

Empty me of anything that
    Could obscure in me what's true;
Fill me with Your Spirit-filled Joy
    To live totally for YOU.

PRAYER FOR THE SICK

May God's Radiant and Comforting Face
    Beam on you today;

May God's Protective and Enduring Love
    Gently light your way;

May God's Redeeming and Sanctifying Grace
    Dwell in your heart to stay;

May God's Peaceful and Strengthening Spirit
    Empower you every day;

May God's Compassionate and Caring Touch
    Bless you through us, we pray.

REFLECTION ON PAIN

P Mixed with the sunshine of our lives
   Comes pain we oft' must bear;
It signals us of *purpose* time
   God calls us to in *prayer*.

A Aware of God, we *affirm* His love
   And special care each day;
Able then to *accept* His Will,
   Our weakness goes away.

I Instead of anxious questioning
   With childish frets and tears,
Invited to His *intimacy*,
   He banishes our fears.

N This *newness* of perspective, hence,
   Brings hope and trust to face
That pain is gainful *nourishment*
   With God's own healing grace.

"From the rising to the setting of the sun is the name of the Lord to be praised."

Psalm 113:3

Seasonal

A CHRISTMAS BLESSING

BLESSINGS be yours in abundance today,

LIGHT of the Infant make bright your life's way;

EMMANUEL, love-gift ever sublime,

SPARK all your nights with a brilliance divine;

SPIRIT most Holy, grant you Spirit Joy,

INCARNATE the hope of Mary's Babe Boy;

NEWNESS be yours through choice gifts from above,

GOD BLESS YOU ALWAYS! I pray now with love.

A CHRISTMAS INVITATION

Reflect with me this twenty-fifth of December,
    this holy event to remember.

Pray with me in praise to God for Mary's Son,
    Who brings true love to everyone.

Sing with me hymns and carols of Christmas peace,
    inspiring hope for wars to cease.

Smile with me in grace-filled merriment and cheer,
    for God reveals His Presence here.

Cry with me over oppression in all lands,
    and bear the grief of wounded hands.

Share with me kind regard for the sick and old,
    that they might know blessings manifold.

Listen with me to the urgings of Jesus' call
    for spreading His Good News to all.

Eat with me at the Eucharistic Table;
    toast the Christ Child in the stable.

Work with me to build a world where peace reigns true,
    through harmony in me and you.

Rejoice with me that Emmanuel's lowly birth
    has touched and blessed our sacred earth.

Let's celebrate Christmas every day,
    especially in all we do and say.

AN AUTUMN REFLECTION

I look out my window in amazement to see
Nature's lips in movement to share God-talk with me.

The warmth from strong sunbeams and brightness of today
Are gentle reminders that night has moved away.

Huge trees, swaying branches, look like stately towers,
While winds breezing 'round them howl sounds of their
    power.

The multi-colored leaves that beautify our earth
Soon leave their high abode to plan for a new birth.

Smooth grass, once green, is burnt with blades now coated
    brown;
Harvest season signals that winter's coming down.

All autumn speaks of change with summer-breaking hands,
Portraying scenes of love in choicest, colored strands.

How very much like life, this vision of fall;
God's everlasting love descends upon us all.

In Jesus, we receive deep warmth and healing light;
Pain and lonely moments move on, as does the night.

Though joys and sorrows paint the leaves on my life's tree,
God's choice of colors blend in perfect harmony.

When youthful health is worn through bodily ill and toil,
God's compassionate care brings supernatural soil.

True growth requires much time and patience to mature;
God's Son endured long trial to death—for life secure.

Help me, dear God, to bring this love scene everywhere;
And bless my autumn life, I pray in praise-filled prayer.

AN EASTER PRAYER

Lord,

       Make my life an *Alleluia,*
           Echoing one long refrain
       With loud blessing and thanksgiving
           To salute Your Holy Name.

       You have conquered death and risen
           Bringing power for life anew;
       At this Easter celebration,
           Take my song of praise to You.

       Place each note of my life's love-tune
           Into special melody;
       Let all hear the Paschal Message
           Through Your Presence lived in me.

       With Your Mother's intercession,
           Help me sing this hymn of praise
       Adding to the *Alleluia*—
           "*Fiat*" now and all of my days.

A WINTER REFLECTION

When snowflakes rapidly fall from the sky
Giving us scenes of white pillars nearby,

Consider taking some into your hand
And with them reflect and pray as you stand.

All of life's sorrows and all piercing pain,
Any big problems that cause you much strain,

Take and form into a snow ball with fun;
Then hold and expose to Jesus, the Sun.

The warmth of His love will melt all away
And you will enjoy God's Peace more each day.

CHRIST IS BORN

When I see Faith lived out
     Where one could easily doubt,
I know that Christ is born.

When I see hopeful peace
     Where trials seldom cease,
I know that Christ is born.

When I see hands that sow
     Where others dare not go,
I know that Christ is born.

When I see feet that trod
     Where paths lead near to God,
I know that Christ is born.

When I see hearts that care
     Where needs uplift in prayer,
I know that Christ is born.

When I see those who teach
     Where others fail to reach,
I know that Christ is born.

When I see friendship true
     Where God brings love anew,
I know that Christ is born.

I see HIS BIRTH in YOU!

JOY-FILLED GREETINGS

Christmas celebrates Christ's birth
Healing Season for true mirth;

Remembrances prompt deep prayer,
In our hearts and hands to share.

See Him in the crib anew;
Tenderly, He blesses you.

Mary gently bids us draw near;
Arms outstretched dispel all fear.

Spirit overwhelms with peace:
Jesus' love will never cease.

Open now my gift of Joy
May you hold Heaven's Baby Boy
In your heart and home always!

"*Happy are they whose way is blameless, who walk in the law of the Lord.*"

Psalm 119:1

Beatitudes

BEATITUDES FOR TEENS

Blessed are the teens who *believe* in God and know that God's Love for them is unconditional, for they possess the Spirit's Gift of **KNOWLEDGE.**

Blessed are the teens who *listen* and respond to the voice of God and their parents rather than be led by peer pressure, for they possess the Spirit's Gift of **COUNSEL or RIGHT JUDGMENT**.

Blessed are the teens who *energize* themselves with the power of the Eucharist for strength in difficult decisions, for they possess the Spirit's Gift of **FORTITUDE or COURAGE.**

Blessed are the teens who *speak* out with conviction when truths of the faith are questioned or challenged, for they possess the Spirit's Gift of **WISDOM.**

Blessed are the teens who *serve* the sick, the elderly, and the needy with kindness and joy, for they possess the Spirit's Gift of **UNDERSTANDING.**

Blessed are the teens who *inspire* others to pray, to receive the sacraments, and to show respect for the Church, for they possess the Spirit's Gift of **PIETY or REVERENCE.**

Blessed are the teens who *name* the dangers of drugs, sex, and alcohol, and resist giving in to them, for they possess the Spirit's Gift of **FEAR OF THE LORD or WONDER or AWE.**

Blessed are the teens who *give* God praise and thanksgiving for all their gifts, especially for life and love, for they possess a **GRATEFUL HEART.**

Teens who live and share these Gifts of the Spirit will be blessed indeed, and will inherit the Kingdom of Heaven.

BEATITUDES OF A CHRISTIAN WOMAN

Blessed is the woman who **BEARS** Christ in her personhood and leads others to give birth to Christ in their hearts, for she possesses. . . . . . . .THE EMBODIMENT OF CHRIST.

Blessed is the woman who **LISTENS** attentively to God's Word and shares the Good News with others, for she possesses. . . . . .THE SPEECH OF CHRIST.

Blessed is the woman who **EMPTIES** herself of useless concerns and focuses on special communion with God and others, for she possesses. . . . . THE UNITY OF CHRIST.

Blessed is the woman who **SEEKS** the strength of the Holy Spirit and perseveres in difficult undertakings, for she possesses. . . . . THE SPIRIT OF CHRIST.

Blessed is the woman who **SERVES** others in Christian stewardship, especially the poor, the sick, and the elderly, for she possesses. . . . THE HEALING POWER OF CHRIST.

Blessed is the woman who **INSPIRES** others with an attitude of prayerful surrender and forgiveness, for she possesses. . . . . .THE PEACE OF CHRIST.

Blessed is the woman who **NURTURES** others with spiritual insight through a deep faith and strong prayer life, for she possesses. . . . . .THE VISION OF CHRIST.

Blessed is the woman who **GIVES** of herself unselfishly to God and others with gratitude and joy for the gift of life, for she possesses. . . . . **THE GENEROSITY OF CHRIST.**

The woman who promotes the kingdom
of Christ on earth, will indeed inherit
the Kingdom of Heaven.

EIGHT BEATITUDES FOR CATECHISTS

Blessed are the Catechists who LISTEN to their students,
    especially those with repeated questions,
For they possess the EARS OF CHRIST.

Blessed are the Catechists who SEE the needs of their students,
    especially those unrecognized by others,
For they possess the EYES OF CHRIST.

Blessed are the Catechists who SPEAK kindly to their students,
    especially those without positive motivation,
For they possess the MOUTH OF CHRIST.

Blessed are the Catechists who TOUCH their students gently,
    especially those who feel stings of home-violence,
For they possess the HANDS OF CHRIST.

Blessed are the Catechists who THINK prayerfully of their
students,
    especially those who don't know God,
For they possess the MIND OF CHRIST.

Blessed are the Catechists who show LOVE to their students,
    especially those with unlovable traits,
For they possess the HEART OF CHRIST.

Blessed are the Catechists who WALK patiently with their students,
	especially those lacking spiritual guidance,
For they possess the FEET OF CHRIST.

Blessed are the Catechists who persevere in their Faith-sharing ministry,
	especially when their efforts seem in vain,
For they possess the HEALING PRESENCE OF CHRIST,
AND THEIRS IS THE KINGDOM OF HEAVEN.

BEATITUDES OF A SISTER

Blessed is your title, Sister, a *unique title*, for it bears your unique relationship with others in a family with siblings; in a community with believers; in a society with diverse backgrounds; and most importantly, in a Religious Institute with consecrated women.

Blessed is your title, Sister, a *revealing title*, for it points to your service to God, the Church, and others. The title outwardly reveals that God has chosen you to be a servant, to carry out His plan to live the Gospel values in the world.

Blessed is your title, Sister, an *identifying title*, for you not only *do* the things of a Sister, but you *are* a Sister. You are one who claims the title of a *religious woman*, promising to live in poverty, chastity, and obedience, with JOY and with an open heart, to share the fruits of your oblation with others for the purpose of leading them closer to Christ.

Blessed is your title, Sister, a *significant title*, for it conveys to the world that you no longer live for yourself, but for others, to teach them that sacrificial giving of oneself has significant value, and that no gift is too great for Christ.

Blessed is your title, Sister, a *sacred title*, for through your personal prayer life and your regard for the sacred truths of our Faith, you are able to inspire others to grow in the understanding and appreciation of the sacredness of God's Word, and the Gift of Life.

Blessed is your title, Sister, a *respectful title*, for when someone addresses you or calls your name, it resonates with a tone of respect. The title distinguishes you from married persons, and sets you apart from the materialism of the secular world.

Blessed is your title, Sister, a *nurturing title*, for it prompts you to share the light of your Baptismal grace with those who are thirsting for the "Living Waters" of the Spirit, and for the nourishment of Communion with their brothers and sisters in Christ.

Blessed is your title, Sister, a *costly title*, for it costs you all that you are and have. It bears a reminder for you to live in total commitment to God, every moment of your life, in imitation of our Brother Jesus, Whose life and death brought redemption and salvation to all of humanity.

> Praise God for the gift of your sacred vocation and for the healing grace to persevere in living out *your identity* as a SISTER! May you continue to serve God and the Church for many years to come, and thus enjoy the KINGDOM OF HEAVEN!

EIGHT BEATITUDES FOR MINISTERING TO THE SICK AND THE ELDERLY

Blessed are you who *listen* to your patients,
      especially those with constant complaints,
For you possess the EARS OF A HEALER.

Blessed are you who *see* the hurts of your patients,
      especially those overlooked by others,
For you possess the EYES OF A HEALER.

Blessed are you who *speak* kindly to your patients,
      especially those plagued by fear and anger,
For you possess the MOUTH OF A HEALER.

Blessed are you who *touch* your patients gently,
      especially those bruised by insensitivity,
For you possess the HANDS OF A HEALER.

Blessed are you who *think* prayerfully of your patients,
      especially those alone and discouraged,
For you possess the MIND OF A HEALER.

Blessed are you who show *love* to your patients,
      especially those with chronic illness,
For you possess the HEART OF A HEALER.

Blessed are you who *walk* tirelessly to your patients,
      especially those with repeated calls,
For you possess the FEET OF A HEALER.

Blessed are you who *persevere* in your ministry,
      especially with compassion to all patients,
For you possess the HEALING PRESENCE OF GOD,
  AND YOURS IS THE KINGDOM OF HEAVEN.

"To you I lift up my soul, O Lord, my God.
In you I trust..."

Psalm 25:1-2

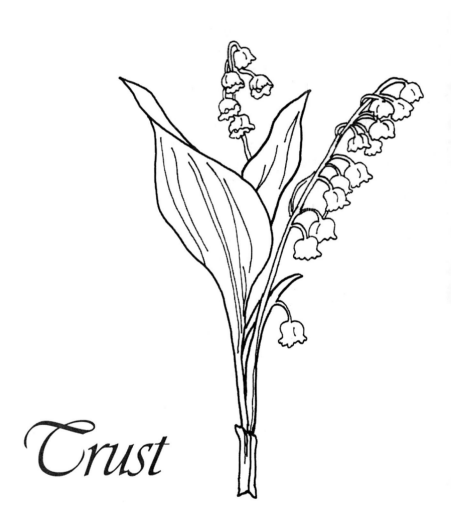

Trust

A PRAYER FOR TRUST

O God, it's dark and I'm scared—
    Grasp tightly my hand;
There's no sight ahead—
    Help me understand.

Show me the way to
    Deeper trust in You;
Anoint me with faith
    To see love anew.

Let me believe that
    Through Your healing touch,
Hope's power will return
    To strengthen me much.

Take hold of all fears,
    The big ones and small;
With You at my side,
    No need is too tall.

Teach me the truth that
    Your grace fills all days;
These special moments
    Can give You more praise.

Thank You for listening
    To my heartfelt prayer;
Thanks, too, for keeping
    This child in Your care.

HEAVEN'S STAR

Jesus, You are the Star
    That shines to give me light,
When night makes difficult
    My balance and my sight.

Jesus, You are the Star
    That guides me on life's way;
You lead me to those paths
    Where I can't go astray.

Jesus, You are the Star
    That lights the darkest skies;
You bring a brilliance strong,
    That opens wide my eyes.

Jesus, You are the Star
    From Heaven's throne above;
You show me how to live
    In true peace, joy, and love.

Jesus, You are the Star
    I will follow always;
Lead me safely onward,
    I ask with trust and praise.

CALLED TO WALK

Lord, I come before You, bruised and bent
To seek some shelter in Your tent.

My walk is rough—the sun beams strong;
I feel great strain—this path is long.

I thirst for drink; my mouth is dry.
I feel a need to cry, O why?

Perhaps the tears will cool my face
So I can carry on this race.

Why, by name, Lord, this choice of me?
Did You forget I am not free?

My life is frail for I've been slain;
I want escape from hurt and pain.

Why urge me on this road for Thee
While there are those less weak than me?

Lord, tell me more about this choice;
I'll be attentive to Your voice.

Child, before approaching Me for hope,
Alone, you dared to climb a slope...
You almost slipped, refusing prayer,
Not trusting in My love and care.
When one is called to walk My way,
The first requirement is to pray.
My call to you made very clear
That such a walk would bring Me near.

Come, take rest, and silence your speech;
Now follow the advice I teach.
Your pilgrim life will only ease
When you turn towards My Spirit Breeze.
The heat of Sun burns, healing true,
For nearness to come over you.
Fear not to grasp the sounds I raise;
You're called to walk in prayerful praise.
Lift heart and hands—surrender wide;
Accept new strength where I abide.
Just give your total self to Me:
You'll walk in JOY, forever free.

I BELIEVE

Dear God,

> I believe that You are with me
> In my climb up mountains tall;
> And I know Your Spirit guides me
> As I cross paths big and small.
>
> I believe You're near me always
> Though it seems You're out of sight;
> Never do You leave my presence,
> You are with me day and night.
>
> I believe that You invite me
> To take shelter in Your heart;
> Without any force upon me,
> You await my willing start.
>
> I believe that You assist me
> In my times of pain and stress;
> And You offer peaceful comfort
> To restore true happiness.
>
> I believe that You are gracious
> As You follow my life's trend;
> Trusting in Your faithful promise,
> I believe Your Love won't end.

IF ONLY I WOULD

If only I would trust in God each moment of my life,
I'd have a strengthening freedom, in spite of trials and strife.

If only I would learn to yield to what God plans for me,
I'd meet my day's encounters with much less anxiety.

If only I would view my pain as splinters from His Cross,
I'd face it as redemptive gain instead of bodily loss.

If only I would focus, more, my vision on God's sight,
I'd see His Love resplendently, though it be dark as night.

If only I would let self go, in God's unfailing power,
I'd have new sense of purpose and find meaning in each hour.

If only I would listen to His sounds in silent prayer,
I'd hear His voice assuring me with comfort, hope, and care.

If only I would patiently give God my self-debris,
I'd walk on smoother paths, and have more room for Him
with me.

If only I would run to heights beyond this time and space,
I'd feel His Holy Spirit's strength support my every race.

If only I would wait in faith for brokenness to mend,
I'd feel Christ's Healing Love in me, with peace that will not
end.

If only I would answer YES—His invite to abide,
I'd live in new-found wholeness, then, for HE WOULD
dwell inside.

ONLY A PRAYER AWAY

When life's road on which you travel seems so winding, long, and steep
And your heart is ever yearning for a faith that's strong and deep,
Remember and be confident—as you come to bumps and bends:
The goal is not beyond your reach, they are challenges God sends,
And know—*We are only a prayer away, my friend, only a prayer away.*

When life's rain is quite torrential, without signs of slowing flow,
Trust that soon you'll see a rainbow, bringing color as you go.
Remember and be confident—downpours of graces abound.
God is watering you with blessings; new creation is around.
And sense—*We are only a prayer away, my friend, only a prayer away.*

When life's winds are fiercely howling and you question: "Is God near?"
Feel the Spirit's strengthening love-touch; God is wiping out all fear.
Remember and be confident—gentle breeze will blow your way
And as those heavy winds calm down, Spirit-peace will fill your day.
Then feel—*We are only a prayer away, my friend, only a prayer away.*

When life's days are dark and cloudy and the sun nowhere in sight,
Jesus does disperse that darkness with His never-fading light.
Remember and be confident—with the Lord there is no night,
All we need is greater trust, and on Him to focus our sight.
Now see—*We are only a prayer away, my friend, only a prayer away.*

When life's journey seems so lonely and you seek some tender care,
Believe that God can fill your heart if you open up in prayer.
Remember and be confident—when in hope and trust we pray,
We receive God's special graces and gain healing strength each day.
Yes—*We are truly only a prayer away, my friend, only a prayer away.*

RECOGNIZE THE LORD

Recognize Me, little child
    In every phase of life;
See Me in your happy times
    As well as those of strife.

Recognize My presence strong
    When trials seem too much;
Feel My overwhelming strength,
    Accept My gentle touch.

Recognize My rays of hope
    Extending healing light;
I have not abandoned you
    Though fog obscures your sight.

Recognize My whispered voice
    Which speaks throughout your pains;
Listen to My message now;
    Its healing power sustains.

Recognize Me in this scene,
    Think not I'm absent here;
Why would I leave as orphan
    You whom I hold so dear?

Recognize Me every day
    In every single place;
Lift your eyes unto My own;
    Behold My love-filled Face.

"*How precious is your kindness,
O God! The children of men take refuge
in the shadow of your wings.*"

Psalm 36:8

Family

A CHILD'S PLEA

Help me grow to truly be
All that God expects of me;
Nothing more and nothing less,
Just to be my very best.

If I stumble low today,
Help me try another way.
Speak kind words but do not preach;
Love is more than what you teach.

When I'm weak and cannot stand,
Stretch your tender, loving hand.
Life is big and I'm so small;
Someday I will grow quite tall.

I'll remember how you cared
Through the patient ways you shared,
And recall the time and place
I saw Jesus in your face.

Then with heartfelt thanks I'll pray
God keep watch o'er you each day;
Blessing you for gifting me
With your best, to help me BE.

ETERNAL LOVE

Know that I am with you always
Death is not the end of me;
I'm in such a peaceful dwelling
Right where God called me to be.

As you mourn for me in sorrow
Wiping tears that steadily flow,
Pray and gratefully remember
That our love will ever grow.

God's love-gift is everlasting
And when life on earth is done,
Love we shared with one another
Joins the Love of God's Own Son.

Parting from you, dearest loved one,
Is for time that is quite brief;
We will celebrate reunion
Without illness, pain, or grief.

Keep on living to the fullest
With the love of God for all;
Be a blessing and a love-gift
To everyone—big or small.

Every time you see the sun shine
With its light upon your face,
Think about my smiling presence
Sending love from Heaven's place.

Love of Jesus, Love Eternal,
Brings true healing in our strife—
Praise for my repose in peace now;
Death has brought me to new life.

MOTHER

Chosen by God to bear me and to share new life on earth,
You gave consent to motherhood, and gifted me with birth.

With your maternal heart and hands, you tendered me with love,
And nurtured deep within my being respect for truths above.

Throughout the years, you challenged me, to live life without
  fear;
Assuring me, during tempest times, that God is always near.

How soothing was your every smile and glance into my eyes—
With gentle, loving touch, you kissed away all fears and cries.

I know that God has graced your walk along His Golden Way,
And pray that rest and peace of His be yours each single day.

May the perpetual light of Christ shine bright upon your face!
And may God bless you with that joy reserved in Heaven's place.

OUR FAMILY PRAYER

Heavenly Father, in Jesus' Name we pray:
Bond our dear family in unity today.

Protect us from all that could hinder true peace;
Direct us to realms where Your blessings increase.

Fortify our faith when life's perils take place
In all our moments we rely on Your grace.

Look kindly upon us and help us to live
With gentle compassion and power to forgive.

Keep us united in Your circle of love
And send forth Your Spirit of Joy from above.

For every gift lavished through Your loving care,
In praise and thanksgiving, we offer this prayer.
Amen.

TO LOVED ONES LEFT BEHIND

Realize that I am with you
Even though you cannot see
I have come to rest in peace now;
God prepared this place for me.

Do not mourn for me in sorrow,
Shedding stream-like tears for long;
Rather, grieve for unkind actions
And for those who live in wrong.

God is love and bids us follow
Paths that lead to truth and life;
Live in prayerful hope and courage,
Mindful that God heals all strife.

Open wide your heart and welcome
Daily challenges your way;
Make God always present in them
Blessing what you do and say.

God's great love is omnipresent
And when life on earth is done,
We continue as beloved
In the arms of God's Own Son.

Now in prayer, look up towards heaven,
Vision of eternal place;
I await you with the angels
In the love-light of God's Face.

"Glorify the Lord with me,
let us together extol his name."

Psalm 34:4

Celebrations

AN ANNIVERSARY PRAYER

Heavenly Father, in Jesus' Name we pray
For our dear friends, this Wedding Anniversary Day.

Grant them many blessings with a faith renewed in You;
Fill their walk together with a love-power ever new.

Gently lead them on life's way; hold high Your guiding light;
Never let them face the dark; keep them in Your sight.

Gift them with Your peace and joy, great happiness and health;
Bless their sons and daughters with unending spiritual wealth.

May their gift of love together last forever and be true;
Reaching peak fulfillment in their unity with You!

A WEDDING REFLECTION

A solemn pledge is made today of everlasting love;
The union of a special pair is sealed from up above.

Marie and Erik have told us their lives will henceforth be
No longer lived as single lives, but in God's unity.

Whatever they will do in life, wherever they will go,
With God to guide them on their way, their love will always grow.

When times are good and roads are smooth, and they are feeling
   glad;
Or travels are more challenging and things appear quite bad,

Their prayerful trust in God will help to carry them anew
To married heights of faithful love and union strong and true.

God's graces fill their every need to bring them strength within,
Enkindle sparks of married love with flames that cannot dim.

God smile His Joy upon their lives through prayers that we now
   send.
May Marie and Erik this day reap blessings without end!

JUBILEE GREETINGS TO A PRIEST

An anniversary is a day
        We set aside each year.
Recalling an experience
        And bringing it right here.

Your day in May, fifty years ago,
        Was quite a special one,
For God chose you to double Him,
        In fashion like His Son.

In counseling others, healing sick,
        Through sacramental power,
You shared your gift of priestly life,
        Anointing every hour.

If you had failed to persevere
        In living out God's Call,
Today we couldn't celebrate
        This jubilee feast at all.

Though you may never realize
        The impact of your life,
Your fifty years in the priesthood
        Freed many from their strife.

I loudly praise the Lord today
        That He's alive in you,
And pray that you'll forever stay
        God's priest, faithful and true.

JUBILEE PRAISE

I give praise for many gifts
    These fifty years have brought,
For God's unceasing mercy
    And all God's Love has wrought.

For gifts of understanding,
    Support and gentle care
That helped me on my faith walk,
    I praise in thankful prayer.

For love of my dear family
    And friendships ever true,
My praise rises like incense
    In prayerful thanks anew.

My heart swells with Spirit Joy
    As I celebrate and pray
To give God praise and glory
    This Golden Jubilee Day!

MY ANNIVERSARY PRAYER

Lord, several years ago, clothed in St. Lucy's attire,
I pledged myself to You—to serve and to inspire.

Accept my humble prayer of gratitude and praise
For all Your wondrous gifts, that graced each of my days.

You've given me the strength to meet my joys and fears
And kept me ever close throughout these passing years.

Your Spirit empowered me that I might truly do
The apostolic work outlined for me by You.

You stretched Your loving hand throughout each day and night
And kept me so secure 'neath Your protective might.

You gave me Mother Mary who interceded, too,
Watching as I journeyed on pathways old and new.

You blessed me with family and friends along my way
To help me reach this milestone; please bless them all I pray.

My heart swells with gladness as I celebrate and pray—
Accept my loud thanksgiving this Anniversary Day!

MY BIRTHDAY PRAYER

O Lord, on my birthday,
       Give me the grace to see
How precious is this life
       You have given to me.

Let me never abuse
       These moments that are mine,
But help me live each day
       As light of Yours to shine.

May my words and good deeds
       Bring Your warmth from above,
To fill the hearts of those
       Who yearn for peace and love.

I give prayerful thanks now
       For all life's gifts from You
And celebrate this day
       With grateful praise anew.

"Show me the way in which I should walk, for to you I lift up my soul."

Psalm 143:8

Surrender

A PROPHET'S PRAYER

Yahweh, I am too young to speak,
My legs tremble, my body's weak.

Yet, Your command now beckons me
To bear Your Word, set captives free.

Convict me with strong faith to know
Just where Your call bids me to go.

Help me be Your messenger true,
So all can see I'm sent by You.

Use my mouth to disclose the wrong,
My hand to pen Your victory song.

Journey with me towards paths of peace;
Let avarice and oppression cease.

Pour forth Your blessings on this day
To all Your people as I pray:

Through me, may hearts come to renew
Their covenant of love with You.

BECAUSE HE CARED

A heavier cross was carried
  Than the one that's mine today:
Jesus was the bearer,
  He shares concern this way
   BECAUSE HE CARED.

The heavily-laden sufferings
  He bore beneath that cross,
Were demonstrations of a *love*
  To compensate a *loss*
   BECAUSE HE CARED.

He freely chose this method
  To teach reality;
And dared me self-surrender,
  For hope-filled liberty
   BECAUSE HE CARED.

Throughout His crucifixion
  And all that pained Him much,
His *yes* response to Abba's Will
  Did bring a healing touch
   BECAUSE HE CARED.

I need to recognize anew
  In every hurt and pain
He never meant to strike me down,
  Or drench me under rain
   BECAUSE HE CARED.

For in His Paschal Mystery,
  He gave His life and love,
And taught me to transcend my ills
  To newer heights above
   BECAUSE HE CARED.

COME, LORD JESUS

Take possession of my heart,
Purify my every part.
Help me make a brand-new start.
Come, Lord Jesus!

Take possession of my eyes,
Lift them towards Your star-lit skies.
Free them from impatient cries,
Come, Lord Jesus!

Take possession of my ears,
Block them from all noisy jeers.
Open them to grace-filled cheers,
Come, Lord Jesus!

Take possession of my lips,
Bless them with Your Sacred Sips.
Seal them from all hurtful slips,
Come, Lord Jesus!

Take possession of my mind,
Empty me of thoughts that bind.
Make them holy, pure, and kind,
Come, Lord Jesus!

Take possession of my all,
Use my gifts, the big and small;
I will answer Your love's Call.
Come, Lord Jesus!

GIVING IN

When life felt harsh and hope was lost,
        In pity, I cried out:
Why is my God so far away?
        Must I more loudly shout?
My efforts seem to be in vain;
        Tears flow into the night.
I'm strongly tempted to give up;
        He seems nowhere in sight.

But then I hear in whispered voice:
        "Child, don't give up, give in.
Remember how on Calvary
        I died so you can win.
Surrender to My Father's Will;
        Accept this special call.
My 'giving in' fulfilled His Plan;
        I bore the cross for all."

I thought about God's gift of love,
        The Paschal Mystery,
And gradually did recognize
        The Healing Victory.
I prayed anew with greater trust
        Repenting for all sin,
And felt a peaceful strength once more
        The moment I gave in.

IN THE HANDS
OF THE POTTER

Lord, You are my Potter
     And I am Your clay;
Soften and shape me
     I fervently pray.
I'm in Your Hands now
     And ask that You do
All that is needed
     To mold me anew.
I offer to You
     This being of mine
To fashion into
     A vessel sublime.
Brush me with the glaze
     Of grace from above;
Fired with Your Spirit,
     Transform me in love.
In Your strong Hands, Lord,
     I'm content to stay
And give prayerful praise
     That I am Your clay.

JESUS, TEACH ME

Jesus, teach me to surrender;
Show me what's Your Holy Will;
Jesus, teach me how to render
Praise and Glory when I'm ill.

It's not easy to be emptied,
Yet, for You to come inside,
I must rid myself of clutter,
To make room so You'll abide.

Jesus, teach me to let go now
Of the stuff I've held too long;
Help me cling to You and Mary;
Jesus, bless me; make me strong.

Crucifixion was Your love-gift
Offered so that I'd be free;
Take this weak and broken body
As a *thank-you note* from me.

Jesus, teach me to share Joy now
'Midst these hours of quiet pain,
Let me feel your healing strength here;
Help me view this loss as gain.

Through and in Your Spirit, Jesus,
Take this praise-message I bring;
To Your honor, thanks, and blessings,
Now and evermore, I sing.

MY DAILY PRAYER

Lord, I thirst for Your Presence,
　　　　　For fuller life in You;
Too oft' I miss our dialog
　　　　　'Midst everything I do.
Quench me with Your grace anew
　　　　　When day seems long and dry,
Keep me ever mindful that
　　　　　You'll always stay nearby.
Lord, I listen to Your Voice now
　　　　　Through varied sounds I hear;
Though some seem faint or muffled,
　　　　　Love echoes loud and clear.
Bless my ears with openness
　　　　　To silence as I pray;
Let them heed Your message true
　　　　　Through how I live today.
Lord, I surrender all to You,
　　　　　My body, mind, and heart;
Take everything I cling to;
　　　　　Accept this willing start.
I offer You in praise and thanks
　　　　　This total self of mine
And ask you to envelop me
　　　　　Into Your Heart Divine.
Lord, help me share Your gentle care
　　　　　With all, along life's way;
Use me to ennoble them
　　　　　Through what I do and say.
Rescue me and those held dear
　　　　　From any hurt and harm,

And shield us in protection
        Beneath Your loving Arms.
Lord, when day ends and night appears
        For my Eternal Place,
Let me celebrate Your Love
        In the vision of Your Face. Amen.

MY OFFERING

Gracious and loving God,
These pains, old and new,
Are lovingly offered
As my gift to You.

Although so unpleasant
And heavy to bear,
They're filled with much meaning
When raised up in prayer.

For comfort and healing
I fervently pray,
But mostly for Your strength
To bear them this day.

May each pain I suffer
Be offered to raise
This gift of myself now,
With love and with praise.

PRAYER TO MARY

To know the secrets of the saints
My heart finds difficult to learn,
Because it hasn't found the spark
Wherein their holy lives did burn.

And so, dear Mary, I have come
To ask your help along my way;
Please listen to this little child
Who seeks your guidance day by day.

Help me to be more faithful now
In spite of all my childish fears;
Teach me the love with which you loved,
That welcomes even painful tears.

Give me the peace and joy of soul
That images your Son's own life,
And flood me with new hope and trust
To see His love in spite of strife.

Do take from me what dims true sight
Because of pride or self-content,
And open wide my eyes to see
God's Holy Will through all I'm sent.

And fashion my whole life anew,
So all who look at me may see
Your portrait and reflection true
Mirrored for eternity.
Amen.

USE ME, LORD

Let me be Your caring face,
Sharing You in every place
Where Your Presence is distant.

Let me be Your loving eyes,
Focusing on lonely cries
Where sight of You remains obscured.

Let me be Your patient ears,
Listening to those sighs and fears
Where Your healing hope is faint.

Let me be Your mouth to speak
Consoling truth to the weak
Where Your words are still silent.

Let me be Your gentle hands,
Serving as the need demands
Where Your touch has not been felt.

Let me be Your sturdy feet,
Walking 'midst the cold and heat
Where Your path is yet unknown.

Let me be Your open heart,
Embracing those kept apart
Where Your love is not alive.

Let me be and let me do
All I can in praise of You.
Use me, Lord, now and always.
Amen.

"Give thanks to the Lord, for he is good,
for his kindness endures forever!"

Psalm 106:1

Symbols

BRIDGES

Of all the bridges you may see,
        The narrow, wide, or tall,
There is a very special one
        Although it is quite small.

You cannot walk or drive on it;
        Just hold it in your hand,
And feel a prayerful presence
        Support you as you stand.

It is a bridge I built for you,
        To help you reach a place
Where hearts and minds unite anew
        And love and care embrace.

However far your travels span
        Across life's land and sea,
Let this bridge be a reminder
        That prayer links you with me.

I pray you, too, be bridge-builder
        With those you meet each day,
And God anoint your efforts true
        Towards His Safe-Passage Way.

Accept this little bridge-gift
        With loving thoughts from me;
May Jesus be your Bridge of Life
        Into eternity!

GOD'S BRIDGES

I cross many bridges while traveling life's ways
And each brings reminders of God's grace-filled days.

Bridges may be of steel, with beams rather tall,
Others are constructed with wooden frame, small.

Bridges may span far across rivers or sea,
Or bring a connection between roads for me.

Bridges may be covered with boards wide and long,
Showing their endurance of winds ever strong.

Bridges carry weights that are heavy or light,
And may connect places in day or at night.

Bridges are God's gifts that allow us to know
Love's outstretched arms extend wherever we go.

Bridges can be people God sends to bring care,
Who willingly help cross life's highway through prayer.

Bridges link yesterday with tomorrow, too,
Connecting God's Mercy with Love-gifts anew.

But the Bridges sturdiest and ever tall
Are Jesus and Mary, most open to all.

May Jesus be our Bridge to the Father above!
May Mary be our Bridge to her Son's Lasting Love!

GOD'S FLOWER

Make me Your flower, dear Lord,
      Fashioned from up above
To spread Your scent and beauty,
      A hybrid of Your love.

The color doesn't matter,
      White, yellow, pink, or blue,
Just make and shape me special,
      A blossom soft and true.

Give to others a new joy,
      Through fragrance rare and sweet;
And drench me with Your Spirit
      To bring to all I meet.

Let me be Your gift, O Lord,
      In lives that need to see
Your Own unique love-sign,
      With this flower made of me.

GOD'S LOVE IN MY CLASSROOM

I SEE Your Love, Lord,
> In the smile on a child's face,
> In this faith-formation place.

I HEAR Your Love, Lord,
> In the laughter that we share,
> In our quiet time at prayer.

I TASTE Your Love, Lord,
> In the snacks the children bring,
> In the sweetness when they sing.

I FEEL Your Love, Lord,
> In the touch of joy You send,
> In the strength that doesn't end.

I HOLD Your Love, Lord,
> In the clasp of a child's hand,
> In the circle where we stand.

I WALK Your Love, Lord,
> In my steps to reach each one,
> In the teachings of Your Son.

I KNOW Your Love, Lord,
> In the gifts of children's love,
> In the blessings from above.

I HAVE your Love, Lord,
> In each moment of this day,
> In gratitude now I pray.

I Praise and thank You, Lord,
For Your unceasing Love!

I SEE LIGHT

I see many lights in the course of a day.
But each seems to flash towards direction *One Way.*
I see red lights and green ones which read stop and go;
And those blinking amber for caution below.

I see lights in the churches on altars and shrines,
Big ones and small ones, in colors of all kinds.
I see lights held still in reverent hand-raise,
Where grateful hearts echo prayerful praise.

I see light bursting from darkness of night,
And light of new day with sun, warm and bright.
I see lights consumed fast, and some burning slow;
Yet, each flickering a powerful glow.

I see light in communion during quiet prayer,
And light signaling God's presence everywhere.
I see light all around me, outside and in;
Light that's bright and light that's dim.

I see light's rays whenever I trod
Where others witness the love of God.
I see light in the faces of new people I meet,
Grown-ups and children, in homes, on the street.

I see in eyes such radiant light,
When someone's wrong is turned to right.
Light of forgiveness, light of good cheer,
Light of understanding, light removing fear.

I see light in community—in compassionate care,
Light in the charity of people who share.
I see light in persevering outreach,
Light in the dedication of those who teach.

Yes, I see light's empowerment in dazzling rays
And feel its effects in so many ways.
I'm thankful to the Light of all light,
Eternal Lord of Power and Might

His love dispelled humanity's night
Through Jesus, His Son, our Redeeming Light.
His Spirit strengthens and enlightens me
To look beyond the self I see.

He bids me now: "Take this Light of Mine
And in your life, let My Light shine."

GOD'S MOSAIC

I am in God's great Mosaic
Pieced within creation's art,
Broken, shaped, and fitted neatly
As God's Own selected part.

Without me there would be missing
In this Master Plan above,
That which God has chosen special
To complete His work of love.

Should I moan for being broken
And begin to question why?
I need only to remember
God's Mosaic from on high.

God's design portrays perfection,
Fashioned, trimmed, and framed just right;
Gently does God's love transform me
Through His Hands of power and might.

Help me, God, and bless my efforts
To accept this shape of me;
Keep my place in Your Mosaic,
Fixed in love eternally.

MY HANDS

I look at my hands with discovery new,
Such awesome gifts they are and yet, challenging, too!

God sealed them forever with His powerful grace
That I might give blessings, and anoint in God's place.

I look at my hands and examine just where
They've extended today God's compassionate care.

Have I made them God's own; have I raised them in prayer?
Were they eager to serve and more willing to share?

I look at my hands; are they quick to forgive?
Or do I pass judgment about how others live?

I'm content to receive what's delightful and free,
But I need to take hold of all God sends to me.

I look at my hands bathed in water run cold,
Accepting the cleansing of stains, recent and old.

How often these hands lack proper care for their skin!
Life, too, calls for treatment when wounded by sin.

I look at my hands; could they pen words to say:
"God's Love is eternal" with conviction this day?

I look at my hands used to take food and eat;
Bread blessed and then broken becomes Communion treat.

Hands must freely unclasp and palms must open wide,
For them to be transformed by Christ's dwelling inside.

When will I look at my hands and see not only mine,
But hands molded with love, formed into Christ's, sublime?

MY NAME

God, our Father, called my name from all eternity
To be among His chosen with marked identity.

He formed me in His image with touch of love divine,
And promised that His Kingdom would rightfully be mine.

At birth, He told the world that I dwelt within His Heart,
And gave me consecration to Him, right from the start.

In waters of my Baptism, His Spirit blessed my name,
Anointing me with power no other one could claim.

My name impels me to witness His truth throughout the land,
In service to God's people, with hope and love in hand.

God asks me to keep holy my name for Him each day,
To let it bring Him glory in all I do and say.

Wherever I may journey, He offers me His grace
And prompts me to let others see Jesus in my face.

I pray for deeper faith now, and courage to proclaim
The Spirit of the Father Who breathed into my name.

O Triune God, stay with me, and grant protection true;
Please seal my name forever with faithfulness to You.

THE PEARL

Lord, in this Pearl that I see
      I've captured anew
A luster and beauty
      Formed only by You.

Help me to keep away
      The sand in life's shell,
So I can see clearly
      Where You choose to dwell.

Let me remember that
      You freely abide
Where clutter of self is
      Removed from inside.

I promise to treasure
      And value with love,
The Pearl of Your Presence,
      Gift sent from above.

REFLECTION ON SHELLS

While walking on the ocean's floor
    One evening in mid-June,
My eyes took notice of the shells
    That lay beneath the moon.
So, one by one, I searched and picked
    And held some in my hands;
Free treasures became mine that day,
    God-sent from soft-beach sands.
How different are the many forms
    Which single out each shell!
What stories of endurance long
    I'd learn if they could tell!
Then, as I held each shell, I thought:
    These gifts from off the sea
Are easily likened to the years
    I've spent in ministry.
Life in the sea of God's vast love
    Brought treasures through this call;
And prayer made smooth the challenges
    To meet storms, big and small.
Just as years of winds and rain
    Helped shape each shell's own face,
So too, have years of joy and pain,
    Brought newness to my place.
It takes an emptied shell to show
    That beauty lies within;
I'm free of sand or clutter small,
    When I avoid all sin.
How very blessed and graced I am
    To lead more hands to raise
In special shell-like fashion, now,
    Their gifts of love and praise.

Dear God, accept this grateful heart
　　And keep me one in Thee.
I thank You for Your blessings
　　In this faith-shared ministry.

ABOUT THE AUTHOR

Sister Marie Rose Roccapriore, M.P.F., is a native of Meriden, Connecticut, and a member of the Religious Teachers Filippini Community, Villa Walsh, Morristown, New Jersey. She holds degrees from Villa Walsh College, Morristown, New Jersey; Notre Dame of Maryland University, Baltimore, Maryland; LaSalle University, Philadelphia, Pennsylvania; and Hartford Seminary, Hartford, Connecticut.

She has taught in elementary schools in New Jersey, Rhode Island, Maryland, Connecticut, and Pennsylvania, and was principal of St. Nicholas of Tolentine School in Philadelphia. Sister Marie was Director of Religious Education, Pastoral Minister, and Coordinator of the Rite of Christian Initiation Ministry (RCIA) in various parishes in Connecticut.

Currently, Sister Marie's apostolate is at St. Thomas Parish, Southington, Connecticut, where she is Director of Religious Education. She also directs *Spirit Joy Children's Music Ministry*, founded by her for the purpose of bringing the Joy of the Holy Spirit to the sick and elderly in hospitals, nursing homes, health-care facilities, and assisted living residences.

About Leonine Publishers

Leonine Publishers LLC makes fine Catholic literature available to Catholics throughout the English-speaking world. Leonine Publishers offers an innovative "hybrid" approach to book publication that helps authors as well as readers. Please visit our web site at www.leoninepublishers.com to learn more about us. Browse our online bookstore to find more solid Catholic titles to uplift, challenge, and inspire.

Our patron and namesake is Pope Leo XIII, a prudent, yet uncompromising pope during the stormy years at the close of the 19th century. Please join us as we ask his intercession for our family of readers and authors.

Do you have a book inside you? Visit our web site today. Leonine Publishers accepts manuscripts from Catholic authors like you. If your book is selected for publication, you will have an active part in the production process. This book is an example of our growing selection of literature for the busy Catholic reader of the 21st century.

www.leoninepublishers.com

CPSIA information can be obtained
at www.ICGtesting.com
Printed in the USA
FFOW01n2033070515
13187FF

9 781942 190097